THE POINT IS YOU ARE ALIVE

Natalie Whittaker is a poet and teacher from South East London. She is the author of two pamphlets: *Shadow Dogs,* and *Tree*, which has also been published in French. Natalie was a London Library Emerging Writer 2020 – 2021.

Also by Natalie Whittaker

Tree   (Verve Poetry Press, 2021)

Shadow Dogs   (Ignition Press, 2018)

CONTENTS

tree

For Ivy and Ruby

ISBN: 978-1-916938-88-5

The author has asserted their right to be identified as the author of this Work in accordance with the Copyright, Designs and Patents Act 1988

Cover designed by Aaron Kent

Edited and Typeset by Aaron Kent

Broken Sleep Books Ltd
PO BOX 102
Llandysul
SA44 9BG

The Point Is You Are Alive

Natalie Whittaker

Broken Sleep Books

some new flats look like **Jenga blocks** against the sky   a man
walks past looking at his phone   not looking at his phone   the
bus to Bellingham rounds the corner   a sign says   *This is a*
Public Space Protection Order Area   Pick up after your dog   Put
your dog on a lead when instructed to do so by an authorised officer
Max 6 dogs   Do not walk more than 6 dogs   dogs have been
causing problems around here   problems beyond imagining   a
woman I know stops and chats with me   I tell her how busy I
am   so busy   so tired   she says   *I'm not surprised   I*
don't know how you do it all   by which I think she means all the
time I spend   telling people how busy   and tired I am   a
fun-size Snickers wrapper skids through full-size leaves   a girl
is sat outside a café   in an orange faux fur jacket   orange faux
fur jacket   leopard print skirt   black DMs   she looks so
confident   and real   I envy people their south-facing balconies
I wish my life contained more south-facing balconies   where are
the pigeons walking   with such purpose

9

NOT AGAIN

When I came home that night you were raving
to the shipping forecast in the kitchen,
moving with the grace of a broken puppet
and wearing the hair of the dog; his brown fur.
I said *you bring me peace like an earthquake.*
You turned on the smashed-up tiles and said *watch*
what happens when one person screams at night
then screamed at the night. The whole city screamed
back; echoes smacking around cars and lampposts.
Only the shaved dog stayed silent. I knew
in the morning the sparrows would drop eggshells
like our thoughts all snappish and empty,
and somewhere a fox was gargling acid
and fishponds reflected the obvious stars.

I watch *Jurassic Park* for what must be the hundredth time
in a packed living room all chairs and floor space taken the
volume is turned right down and everyone's talking over it but
I fill in the plot and can quote all the lines *maybe across the belly
spilling your intestines the point is you are alive when they start
to eat you* I say the seatbelts in the helicopter don't work this
is called foreshadowing a mosquito is silent trapped in amber
and stuck with a needle *spared no expense* Kate brings in some
beers stands in front of the screen and by the time our bottles
are empty Nedry's driving through driving rain in a yellow
mac towards blindness all security systems down *you didn't
say the magic word* and Kate says we don't need the sound on do
we you know it all and I suppose I do I know what it's like to
climb an electric fence and be too scared to let go too scared
to jump off to hold on tighter even as the siren is wailing a
warning to let it surge to explosion *the point is you are alive
when they start to eat you* Dr Malcom is silent bleeding on the
back of a jeep mouthing *must go faster must go faster* and I
know how it feels to hold a shattered windscreen up against
the teeth and breath so close in the night to flail a flare in the
darkness a distraction and if you ask do I breed raptors I'll
nod and wear a white coat and say yes I breed raptors my
velociraptors hatching from their eggs all crying and claws and
I cradle them even as I hate them and they grow learn to
open doors doors I've tried to keep shut stalk around unlit
kitchens snorting and purring my terror reflected in a stainless
steel cabinet trapped and tap tap tapping a ladle a distraction
but *life* they say *life finds a way* you just have to wait for the
helicopter to lift you off the island

MOSS

That winter I was under the influence
of moss. The first sign was a taste
for sour milk; I'd watch it cloud and spore

in tea, its spiral galaxy expanding.
Next, I decorated the flat with green doormats
and X-rays of smokers' bronchial tubes.

I imagined the countryside, where moss
would bloom over wells, stone bridges and troughs;
a place where I could let the moss

moss over me. Instead, I slept in the shower;
curled around the plughole in a damp bikini,
fingering clumps of pubic hair. I brewed soup

in old plant pots. Threaded spinach
between my teeth. Powdered my cheeks with mould.
I longed to be lichen, to breathe salt air

until the nightmares of limpets began;
their radulae rasping my flesh from rock
then leaving, returning to their home scars.

A chicken box ricochets down the aisle: *Hot
& Tasty - just the way you like it!* Tonight,
the pigeon-shit town washes by, under a cold
and tasteless sky; this place where we've wasted
our lives like two spiders circling a sink.
And the plastic seats swing through the streets
and the STOP button shrieks at you to STOP,
but the silver trace of everyone's day has fogged
the top deck windows, and you dare to write
your name in that breath, that's censed a hundred
rain-bedazzled hoods; knowing that the cost
of those letters in condensation – your
wet syllables ghosting sodium light –
is the use of all of those strangers' breaths.

THE RING-NECKED PARAKEETS OF SOUTH EAST LONDON

are screaming and green;
in their hundreds they lift

from fired-up trees
and flee over luminous joggers,

reined lurchers, a lake,
into a highlighter-pink sky,

as beyond park gates, rudeboys rev
their snarling engines.

And if night starts anywhere, it's here:
the earth leaching light from the sky

as the sun's dusty projector bulb dies.
We splash through dark that pools on paths

and run from the evening that roosts,
silencing the suburbs.

the night someone threw a brick   through the windscreen of
the bus   all eight feet of glass burst at once   like a spit bubble
shivers whispered down the aisle   sparkled on the front seats
and in the silence   that followed   I checked I was alive   the
bus exhaling hot exhaust   I was still alive   three rows from the
front   I was still alive   on Dartford Hill   did I want to be alive
and what is this life   if not a brick through the windscreen   of
every day   I wanted to be the brick   and the glass   slivers so
precious   they should be picked   from the plastic floor   with
white gloves   under the LED strip lights   those ugly stars   but
splinters of me would remain   even after the repair shop   the
depot   even weeks later   the bus back in service   I'd be there
being ground down under buggy wheels   that squeal like pigs
my crushed silver   reflected   in a convex mirror

BAIT

He loved to tell the story of the time he carefully spooned
a pint of maggots through the letterbox
of the *miserable cow* who lived three floors down.

I'd imagine them clagging the black bristles like eyelashes,
their sawdust-coated bodies, rainbow-dyed from the tackle shop,
crying onto her doormat. I'd wonder

how long it took for their scattered colours
to fill her flat, whether they got as far as her toothbrush,
her pillow, before she got back, and I hated

the idea of him doing that, and being my dad.
I sat half-impressed, half-terrified, hooked
in a room full of eyes that watched but did not blink.

BOAT PARTY

The Thames is electric and the evening drunken; the lighting rig spinning pink and green out onto the river; every highlight on the water like a fag butt briefly sparkling then trod on, every ashy constellation lost in others. Below decks, it's hip-hop vs RnB and hip-hop is winning, just. We pass under Hungerford Bridge and for a few seconds worry that people will gob on our heads and in our pints, but then, in the space above a paddle steamer moored on the Embankment, the Houses of Parliament put their hands in the air, raise gun fingers to the sky, and some guy gives the finger to the building in general and shouts *fuck those pricks!* and we all laugh and repeat *fuck those pricks!* but I'm sure everyone is thinking of a different, individualised prick or set of pricks. We chug on into a Sex on the Beach-coloured sunset, and the moon is raw like a spot of flesh under peeled sunburn, and inside the crowd hammers on the low gilt ceiling as a track drops, and later there'll be ringing in ears and later there'll be strobes like lightning.

WHITSTABLE

Do you remember how we stumbled
down that tipsy pebble beach,
and cried out at the tilting night sky
that shook silver coins into the ocean,
a spilt glass of black wine. Or how
the constellation of a ship went by:
white-red-white. Or how, that night,
our tongues oiled with happiness, we shied
pebbles at the sea, but threw to miss.

TO THE GIANT GROUND SLOTH IN THE NATURAL HISTORY MUSEUM

You surprised me, lurking in a gallery
of framed plesiosaurs and ichthyosaurs
- those fossils like fish bones on tinfoil -
but pleasantly; not like the stranger
in a stained tracksuit who flashed his cock
in an underpass when I was fourteen.
They've given you a tree to embrace.
It's branchless; you caress its smooth bark
between broad claws and stumpy legs
cast in plaster under Victorian arches.
Evolution reduced you; forced you
to climb trees you once stood eye-high to.
Evolution exhausted you. Your shadow
rests on bricks the shade of old urinals.

GUY'S HOSPITAL, OCTOBER 2015

In the waiting room a game show called *The Edge*
combines bowling skills with general knowledge.
Nobody watches or changes the channel.
I carry a chewed polystyrene cup

to the ward that's wired with orange poison.
There's a woman who looks worse than you,
wearing a cold cap that fuses *Tron*
with 50s swimwear fashion. Her husband

loiters. I think *please never let this happen*
– I give you water - *to me*. Your fingernails
are gone. Outside the window, sunlight streams
through The Shard and London Bridge Station.

the first time I saw my own ghost   I had a whole tube carriage to myself   dragging back from a weekend   that had ended early   it was Sunday morning   my nerves fried onions   I'd been dragging a small plastic case   with wheels that cried   like dying cats   now just a rocking   weight between my knees   the window opposite flashed   a blank phone screen   behind my eyes   my brain cramped   in the small bone case   I'd been dragging around for years   and that grey reflection appeared disappeared   reappeared   against a black wall   held her skull in her hands   an onion   I knew I'd keep dragging   back down the same tunnels   back down the same tunnels   for years   wiping the same grit from my eyes

THE CORNER CAFE

I'm sat outside *The Corner Cafe*, which I still pronounce *caff*, not *ca-fay*. A siren scatters pigeons and I have to keep shifting the table and my position at the table to keep my face in the sun. The sun is reading me over the shoulder of a tower block, like the one I didn't grow up in, but my dad did, and that I visited every Sunday for twelve years; where we'd go up in the steel lift and my nan would say *mind the corners girls, there's tiddles in the corners,* because men pissed in the corners. I've finished my panini, and it's not a toasted sandwich, it's a *panini*. A van hesitates before taking a sunlit parking space, and I let the waitress take my plate. My first job was washing plates, which applies to most people, I know, but I'm the only person I know who was dropped off at Oxford in a Transit van. And when I was a baby in that flat, my nan would wash me in the sink, and put me on the side to dry, like a plate. For a minute the traffic goes loud, like some cars all suddenly escaped from somewhere. And then my mum calls my phone, and I know that I have that voice, like a seagull circling a tip; and I'll always feel this little bit ugly and broken inside, like a washing machine left out on the street, but now I'm writing that down, I'm not reading *The Sun*, or eating my tea off a tray, and now I'm forcing a point, and I suppose what I'm trying to make myself say is something like *sometimes I don't know what to say.*

STAY

A dog's shadow crosses the park, let loose
off its black lead it sniffs and is sole
eyewitness to empty booze bottles
tangled in nettles; the necromancy
and parliament of the previous evening
where we exercised our shadow dogs
on the slopes up to the smashed-glass hothouse,
fearing their size in the heartthrob dusk,
their stilt legs stretched and monstrous
as the sun sat obediently down.

stars are clichés * so here are some stars * look at the beautiful
stars * their light * dreams are clichés * so here are my dreams
* O let me tell you about my horrible dreams * their lack of light
* nights fried and chopped * an onion is too much of a mouthful
* so put an onion in your mouth * put an onion in your mouth
* in a dream * under sweating stars * peel back the layers from
stars * and you will be * so beautiful * a dream * smelling
of light * and onions *

ACCIDENT

It was the only time I ever heard him say it –
or anything like it – bellowing testosterone
road rage, red-faced at the kerb of a flyover:
Fucking prick what were you trying to do?
I nearly went into the side of you!
Learn how to drive you fucking mug!

And then, the impact, spat across the tarmac:

I've got three kids in the back of this car
who I love more than anything else in the world!
He slammed back into the driver's seat,
incandescent in the rear view mirror.
And we drove off.
Love. My heart inflated like an airbag.

sometimes it's like   you're in a burning plane   and I'm in the
control tower   that's also on fire   and it's all jagged metal and
red flashing lights   wires sparking and dead co-pilots   and
we're screaming mayday   over   mayday   the air is full of
noises   and I want you   to jump out of those flames   fall
through cloud   without a parachute   hurtling   towards
a spinning map of Northern Europe   London flaring like a
struck match   arteries of light around a suburb   to land in
a cool garden   your head on the ground   insects scurrying
down your ear canals   **listen**   the air is full of noises

FENCED

The smell of next door's dog shit slinks
through football-smashed fence panels,
stubborn as South London self-esteem; *no
one likes us, we don't care.* Their kids
don't care for privacy; trampolining
up against the back wall, sniggering
as I sunbathe. Our garden is stitched
with weeds and, no, I realise, I don't care.
A few fences over, a man calls his daughter
with my name, and all my atoms slip
like Adidas bottoms on a leatherette settee.
Bluebottles thread the humming blades of grass,
and looking up through sunlight's needles
I wonder how much height of sky we own.

I'm struggling with my driving instructor   she looks like a
woman I hate   the woman my friend stood up for   said *she's
South American   she's fiery*   as if that made it all ok   that was
a red light   but long before that happened   I knew it would
happen   it was always going to happen   so I need to be like a
tiny Buddha   or like the website *Tiny Buddha*   that I read in
bed some mornings   and accept that sometimes time   is more
like a spiral   or a roundabout   than a straight line   and that I'll
keep coming back to the same mistakes   like ignoring red lights
arguing in the streets   outside of Indian restaurants   overtaking
without indication   petty revenges   undue hesitation   holding
life on the clutch   I have too much trust in people   who drive
cars   sometimes I look at people in cars   and wonder what
the rest of their bodies look like   when they're not sat in cars
sometimes I get an urge to run   after people in cars   I like to be
one person   in a queue of people in cars   it feels good to be part
of something   even just traffic   at a **red light**

WINTER LANDSCAPE WITH SKATERS

An unwanted dog has been painted out;
whitewashed, like my memory of my dad saying
if you'd been a dog, I would have drowned you at birth.

The ghost dog is still there beneath the ice;
it barks up at the blades of skaters
as they cross the frozen surface of the lake.

COMMON

New College, Oxford, second year 'halfway dinner'; by now, I'm nearly halfway comfortable with being here, but then Michael D who studies Theology announces at me – and the table in general – *Your voice has a very common twang.* For a few seconds I burn silence, then make light – *It might be common in Bexleyheath, but it's pretty rare round here!* Common. Common like there's loads of me, the loose change of me rattling around in pockets; bits of me down the backs of sofas, a smear of me trodden into carpet. So I take offence, then smile and take drinks in a candlelit common room

and eighteen months later I'm standing with the man who runs a graduate training scheme in advertising, and he's telling me: *You're so surprising, so refreshing; you sound like you should be working in JD Sports or something, then I find out you went to Oxford!* then he frowns and says he's *worried* – had I *taken offence?* and I wonder how much offence one person is supposed to take, and just how common this feeling is.

BLACKHEATH

Running across the dark heath in bare feet,
missing broken glass through drunken luck
was like everything else between us:
the dare, the laugh, the risk, the knowing
that we were only one step from pain.
Pissing about at the end of summer's
hottest day. The sudden giant drops of rain.

DEEP FIELD

A moth's wing stammered in the air vent
I unzipped on one side of the bell tent.

Tea lights spent their carbon in a lantern
that panicked stars onto the canvas.

Outside, deep field, you pointed at a moon
so real your finger came back dusty.

We stared like telescopes at our past -
that dark spot encrusted with galaxies.

sometimes the bubble bursts   so completely   that you realise
it wasn't a bubble   after all   but a bomb   you'd been living
in   for all this time   like a piece of faulty wiring   unaware of
your own role   in the explosion   sparking like an idiot   as
component pieces   chain react   all around you   and as the
whole country steps inside   to watch the hailstones detonate
against the windows   to wash their hands   to the chorus   of The
Killers   Mr Brightside   to see their jobs   family relationships
sense of reality   all dissolve   in a **March** wind   you feel a bit
better   because you were ahead of this curve   had practised
this devastation   for some time   going into your cage   doing
just fine

Tree

TREE

on the path to the station
there's a tree   that marks the seasons
look baby   blossom
look baby   leaves
look baby   autumn
next year I'll show you autumn   and it will be so beautiful
the world is   so beautiful
I will show you

one day I wake up   and it's November
bare branches are faulty umbilical cords
failing to implant the sky

CALENDAR

one day I wake up
and it's November
you're not coming back

I start a new job
scrape ice from my windscreen
for the first time this year

yesterday it was June
sunlight through cherry trees

SANDS

one night   it is November   I steer headlights through drizzle
pull up outside a church   that's switched off   in the dark

across a car park of puddles   a community hall squats   like a
secret shame   its orange striplights   draw five broken moths
our wings torn off

Deren calls us all hun   says thanks for coming hun   pours
tea from a cheap white kettle   as we introduce ourselves   to
ourselves   ugly shadows   sleepless   post baby bodies   with
no babies

we sit in a circle   of plastic chairs   stare down at Ugg boots
stained by rain   and talk about our babies

Carly talks about her Evie's grave   the fairy lights   so she
wouldn't be in the dark

Vicky hasn't slept in her own bed   hasn't spoken to her father
since giving birth   she has a holdall and friends' sofas   she is
nineteen

I talk about not having a photo of her face   not holding her at the
time   letting them take her too soon   how four days later   we
went back to the hospital   had her brought up from the morgue
so we could name her

Tasha says mental health services are shit   they just give you
drugs or section you   put you in a room where the curtains are
held on by magnets   says of course I'm suicidal   my baby died

and we smile   because we know   we have to meet in back
rooms at night   broken moth women   swept out of hospitals
and waiting rooms   sedated   or trapped in wardrobes
panicking against the doors

THE FIRST WEEK

interflora deliver
three identical bereavement bouquets
white and green
within a week   the lilies die
their leaves spawn small black flies

in the kitchen   I put away the pans
and a blood clot pushes out of me
like a ragged rotten plum
into maternity tracksuit bottoms

the same night   my milk comes in
breasts are sauna stones   tears are steam
I slide cabbage leaves
into a maternity bra
go to bed   sweat into cabbage leaves
white and green
on the wall   there are small black flies

WHAT TO EXPECT WHEN YOU'RE EXPECTING

the book you bought for me
one sunny afternoon

it was June

      by September
you'd hidden it in the loft

16:44

morphine dragged me under a wave
away from the white shore

where my girl lay sleeping

she was a chipped blue pebble
on a frozen beach

05:07

the tide washes back in   strands me alone
on absorbent white sheets

my chipped heart   has been wheeled away
seabirds have pecked   at my wrists   my eyes

DEPARTURES

1.

we leave the hospital   without our baby   try to drive   out of
the car park   but the barrier is down   I push a ticket   into
the machine   stay duration   24 hours   pay ten pounds eighty
but the barrier   stays down   we reverse   ask the man   can
we please   leave the car park   leave the hospital   without
our baby   the barrier   is down   pay ten pounds eighty   we
leave the car park   and a motorway   is lowered   in front
of us   we have to drive on it   lights swell   on the Dartford
Bridge   we've left our love   our baby   in a morgue   the
night is lowered   in front of us   it stays down

DEPARTURES

2.

we leave the funeral   without our baby
leave her in a white coffin   one in a row
of ten white coffins   a hospital funeral
with nine other babies

                                    we couldn't face
the leaflets   making arrangements
we leave the funeral   without her ashes
we're told there wouldn't be enough of her
to hold on to

DEPARTURES

3.

I watched her birth   her death   in your eyes
my love   how you flinched
turned from her red silence   to look at me
nailed to pain

              when we were young
we thought departure   meant leaving on a train
you waiting on a platform   refusing to look away
until the rails   dragged me out
to flooded fields   the cord between us
so fragile

the moon as an eye stitched open   the moon as a wheel   rolling
my body over rubble   in a wooden cart   the moon as a silver head
dripping molten   over what it cradles   the moon as drawing your
face   then obscuring your face   the moon as having something
small to look after   the moon as a ghost   washed with milk   on
a cold night   the moon as my face   obscured by milk   the moon
as a white face   washed by nurses   on a cold night

TEACHING GCSE ENGLISH

now   there are landmines
waiting under fields   I once owned

thou womb of death

the tight red rope of love

burnt her inside out of course

have plucked my nipple from his boneless gums
            and dash'd the brains out

they detonate
where everything is already broken

LITTLE HERMIT CRAB

you washed from my womb
on a tide of blood

found the blue shell
of a blanket

your tiny hand curled
on the beach of me

white sands shifted
fell away

TIDES

I stand naked   on a black beach
hacked   by white water

the tide crashes in
carries ghosts of fish
that bite the skin from my feet

inside me   a tide turns
spiral arteries   are dying polyps
bleached corals   on a calcified reef

PHANTOM KICKS

my womb shrinks
to the size of a fist

my womb is a fist

CLOCKS

one morning I wake up   and it's November
I stay in bed until it gets dark   it's still November
I'm sure yesterday was June

the clocks have gone back one hour
it's not enough   I need six months
I'm sure yesterday was June

the parks are spitting out fireworks
a bomb has gone off inside me

GOOGLE SEARCH HISTORY

Q   insufficient endovascular cytotrophoblast invasion in spiral arteries

Q   early onset fetal growth restriction

Q   reverse umbilical cord flow causes

Q   survival rate at 24 weeks gestation

Q   trauma counselling

Q   eltham crematorium funeral for babies

Q   early onset iugr

Q   gelatinous placenta ultrasound

Q   when does placental implantation occur

Q   fetal vascular malperfusion

Q   first period after stillbirth

Q   conceiving again after stillbirth

Q   aspirin to increase placental blood flow

Q   guarded outcome meaning

Q   oligohydramnios

Q   24 week stillborn baby pictures

Q   does stress cause stillbirth

Q   how long to grieve a baby

TREE

medical students perch around the room
drawn to our rare   and bitter fruit

the consultant sketches   winter branches
in biro blue   to explain what connects

me to you   what's not getting through

SPRING

in a contagion   of blossom

a pink blooming   pandemic

I switch the radio on

a beat says   *mum*

live   live   live

IVY

Your birth should have killed me.
Just seconds after we'd split into our two
new, separate universes, I was wheeled
away from you, to be stitched up, transfused.

We cheated Death that day, my girl;
slipped his grasp in the place
where he'd already tried to kill me once.

Sewn back together, I held your soft weight
on my chest. Strong vine. Perennial.
A spring day. From that hospital bed
I rose from the dead, with you in my arms.

ACKNOWLEDGEMENTS

The sequence 'Tree' was first published in *Tree* (Verve Poetry Press, 2021)

Other poems in this collection were first published in *Shadow Dogs* (ignition Press, 2018), *bath magg, Poetry News, The Valley Press Anthology of Prose Poetry, Poems for the NHS at 70, #MeToo: A Women's Poetry Anthology, Brittle Star, The Result is What you see Today: Poems About Running* and *We've Done Nothing Wrong. We've Nothing to Hide: The Verve Anthology of Diversity Poems.*

The line 'the point is you are alive when they start to eat you', along with other lines in *I watch Jurassic Park* is taken from Jurassic Park (screenplay by David Koepp).

The line 'if you'd been a dog they would have drowned you at birth' is from *Knives Out* by Radiohead.

teaching GCSE English contains quotations from the following GCSE set texts: William Shakespeare's *Macbeth* and *Romeo and Juliet*, J.B. Priestley's *An Inspector Calls* and Gillian Clarke's *Catrin.*

LAY OUT YOUR UNREST